HYENAS

Maddie Gibbs

PowerKiDS
press™

New York

Published in 2011 by The Rosen Publishing Group, Inc.
29 East 21st Street, New York, NY 10010

First Edition

Editor: Amelie von Zumbusch
Layout Design: Greg Tucker

Photo Credits: Cover, pp. 9, 17, 21, 24 (top left) Shutterstock.com; pp. 5, 13 Hemera/Thinkstock; pp. 7, 11, 23, 24 (bottom left, bottom right) iStockphoto/Thinkstock; pp. 15, 19, 24 (top right) Anup Shah/Photodisc/Thinkstock.

Library of Congress Cataloging-in-Publication Data

APR 1 9 2011

Gibbs, Maddie.
  Hyenas / Maddie Gibbs. — 1st ed.
    p. cm. — (Safari animals)
  Includes index.
  ISBN 978-1-4488-2506-6 (library binding) — ISBN 978-1-4488-2598-1 (pbk.) —
ISBN 978-1-4488-2599-8 (6-pack)
  1. Hyenas—Juvenile literature. I. Title.
  QL737.C24G53 2011
  599.74'3—dc22
                                2010018770

Manufactured in the United States of America

CPSIA Compliance Information: Batch #WW11PK: For Further Information contact Rosen Publishing, New York, New York at 1-800-237-9932

CONTENTS

Hyenas are strong animals.
They are smart, too.

Hyenas have sharp teeth. They have very strong **jaws**.

7

Hyenas have big ears. This helps them hear well. They also have a good sense of smell.

9

Several kinds of hyenas live on Africa's **savannas**.

11

This is a spotted hyena.
Spotted hyenas are the
largest kind of hyena.

Spotted hyenas are known for making a loud cry that sounds like laughter.

15

Spotted hyenas live in groups, called **clans**.

Baby hyenas are called **cubs**. At first, cubs drink their mothers' milk. Later, they eat meat.

19

Hyenas are good
hunters. They eat many
kinds of animals.

Hyenas also steal kills
from other animals.
They eat dead
animals they find, too.

23

Words to Know

clan

cubs

jaws

savanna

Index

Web Sites

Due to the changing nature of Internet links, PowerKids Press has developed an online list of Web sites related to the subject of this book. This site is updated regularl Please use this link to access the list:
www.powerkidslinks.com/safari/hyenas/